POST-SYNODAL APOSTOLIC EXHORTATION

QUERIDA AMAZONIA

OF THE HOLY FATHER
FRANCIS

TO THE PEOPLE OF GOD
AND TO ALL PERSONS OF GOOD WILL

D1377511

QUERIDA AMAZONIA

THE BLESSED AMAZON

APOSTOLIC EXHORTATION

POPE FRANCIS

Our Sunday Visitor
Huntington, Indiana

Apostolic Exhortation © 2020 Libreria Editrice Vaticana
Vatican City

25 24 23 22 21 20   1 2 3 4 5 6 7 8 9

ISBN: 978-1-68192-688-9 (Inventory No. T2562)
eISBN: 978-1-68192-689-6
LCCN: 2020932958

Cover design: Amanda Falk
Cover art: Jesus Teaches the People by the Sea, illustration for "The Life of
Christ," c. 1886–96 (opaque watercolor over graphite on gray wove
papererboard), by James Jacques Joseph Tissot (1836–1902) / French
Purchased by Public Subscription / Bridgeman Images
Interior design: Amanda Falk

TABLE OF CONTENTS

CHAPTER FOUR
AN ECCLESIAL DREAM

• • •

CONCLUSION

1. The beloved Amazon region stands before the world in all its splendor, its drama and its mystery. God granted us the grace of focusing on that region during the synod held in Rome from last October 6–27 [2019], which concluded by issuing its final document, *The Amazon: New Paths for the Church and for an Integral Ecology.*

The significance of this exhortation

2. During the synod, I listened to the presentations and read with interest the reports of the discussion groups. In this exhortation, I wish to offer my own response to this process of dialogue and discernment. I will not go into all of the issues treated at length in the final document. Nor do I claim to replace that text or to duplicate it. I wish merely to propose a brief framework for reflection that can apply concretely to the life of the Amazon region a *synthesis* of some of the larger concerns that I have expressed in earlier documents, and that can help guide us to a harmonious, creative and fruitful reception of the entire synodal process.

3. At the same time, I would like to officially present the final document, which sets forth the conclusions of the synod, which profited from the participation of many people who know better than myself or the Roman Curia the problems and issues of the Amazon region, since they live there, they experience its suffering and they love it passionately. I have preferred not to cite the final document in this exhortation, because I would encourage everyone to read it in full.

4. May God grant that the entire Church be enriched

and challenged by the work of the synodal assembly. May the pastors, consecrated men and women and lay faithful of the Amazon region strive to apply it, and may it inspire in some way every person of good will.

Dreams for the Amazon region

5. The Amazon region is a multinational and interconnected whole, a great biome shared by nine countries: Brazil, Bolivia, Colombia, Ecuador, Guyana, Peru, Suriname, Venezuela, and the territory of French Guiana. Yet I am addressing the present exhortation to the whole world. I am doing so to help awaken their affection and concern for that land which is also "ours," and to invite them to value it and acknowledge it as a sacred mystery. But also because the Church's concern for the problems of this area obliges us to discuss, however briefly, a number of other important issues that can assist other areas of our world in confronting their own challenges.

6. Everything that the Church has to offer must become incarnate in a distinctive way in each part of the world, so that the Bride of Christ can take on a variety of faces that better manifest the inexhaustible riches of God's grace. Preaching must become incarnate, spirituality must become incarnate, ecclesial structures must become incarnate. For this reason, I humbly propose in this brief exhortation to speak of four great dreams that the Amazon region inspires in me.

7. *I dream of an Amazon region that fights for the rights of the poor, the original peoples and the least of our brothers and sisters, where their voices can be heard and their*

dignity advanced.

I dream of an Amazon region that can preserve its distinctive cultural riches, where the beauty of our humanity shines forth in so many varied ways.

I dream of an Amazon region that can jealously preserve its overwhelming natural beauty and the superabundant life teeming in its rivers and forests.

I dream of Christian communities capable of generous commitment, incarnate in the Amazon region, and giving the Church new faces with Amazonian features.

CHAPTER ONE

• • •

A SOCIAL DREAM

8. Our dream is that of an Amazon region that can integrate and promote all its inhabitants, enabling them to enjoy "good living." But this calls for a prophetic plea and an arduous effort on behalf of the poor. For though it is true that the Amazon region is facing an ecological disaster, it also has to be made clear that "a true ecological approach always becomes a social approach; it must integrate questions of justice in debates on the environment, so as to hear both the cry of the earth and the cry of the poor."[1] We do not need an environmentalism "that is concerned for the biome but ignores the Amazonian peoples."[2]

Injustice and crime

9. The colonizing interests that have continued to expand — legally and illegally — the timber and mining industries, and have expelled or marginalized the indigenous peoples, the river people and those of African descent, are provoking a cry that rises up to heaven:

> "Many are the trees
> where torture dwelt,

11

and vast are the forests
purchased with a thousand deaths."[3]

"The timber merchants have members of
	parliament,
while our Amazonia has no one to defend her ...
They exiled the parrots and the monkeys ...
the chestnut harvests will never be the same."[4]

10. This encouraged the more recent migrations of the indigenous peoples to the outskirts of the cities. There they find no real freedom from their troubles, but rather the worst forms of enslavement, subjection, and poverty. Those cities, marked by great inequality, where the majority of the population of the Amazon region now live, are witnessing an increase of xenophobia, sexual exploitation, and human trafficking. The cry of the Amazon region does not rise up from the depths of the forests alone, but from the streets of its cities as well.

11. There is no need for me to repeat here the ample diagnoses presented before and during the synod. Yet let us at least listen to one of the voices that was heard: "We are being affected by the timber merchants, ranchers and other third parties. Threatened by economic actors who import a model alien to our territories. The timber industries enter the territory in order to exploit the forest, whereas we protect the forest for the sake of our children, for there we have meat, fish, medicinal plants, fruit trees. ... The construction of hydroelectric plants and the project of waterways has an impact on the river and on the land. ... We are a region of stolen territories."[5]

12. My predecessor Benedict XVI condemned "the devastation of the environment and the Amazon basin, and the threats against the human dignity of the peoples living in that region."[6] I would add that many of these tragic situations were related to a false "mystique of the Amazon." It is well-known that, ever since the final decades of the last century, the Amazon region has been presented as an enormous empty space to be filled, a source of raw resources to be developed, a wild expanse to be domesticated. None of this recognizes the rights of the original peoples; it simply ignores them as if they did not exist, or acts as if the lands on which they live do not belong to them. Even in the education of children and young people, the indigenous were viewed as intruders or usurpers. Their lives, their concerns, their ways of struggling to survive were of no interest. They were considered more an obstacle needing to be eliminated than as human beings with the same dignity as others and possessed of their own acquired rights.

13. Certain slogans contributed to this mistaken notion, including the slogan "Don't give it away!,"[7] as if this sort of takeover could only come from other countries, whereas in fact local powers, using the excuse of development, were also party to agreements aimed at razing the forest — together with the life forms that it shelters — with impunity and indiscriminately. The original peoples often witnessed helplessly the destruction of the natural surroundings that enabled them to be nourished and kept healthy, to survive and to preserve a way of life in a culture which gave them identity and meaning. The imbalance of power is enormous; the

weak have no means of defending themselves, while the winners take it all, and "the needy nations grow more destitute, while the rich nations become even richer."[8]

14. The businesses, national or international, which harm the Amazon and fail to respect the right of the original peoples to the land and its boundaries, and to self-determination and prior consent, should be called for what they are: *injustice and crime*. When certain businesses out for quick profit appropriate lands and end up privatizing even potable water, or when local authorities give free access to the timber companies, mining or oil projects, and other businesses that raze the forests and pollute the environment, economic relationships are unduly altered and become an instrument of death. They frequently resort to utterly unethical means such as penalizing protests and even taking the lives of indigenous peoples who oppose projects, intentionally setting forest fires, and suborning politicians and the indigenous people themselves. All this [is] accompanied by grave violations of human rights and new forms of slavery affecting women in particular, the scourge of drug trafficking used as a way of subjecting the indigenous peoples, or human trafficking that exploits those expelled from their cultural context. We cannot allow globalization to become "a new version of colonialism."[9]

To feel outrage and to beg forgiveness
15. We need to feel outrage,[10] as Moses did (cf. Ex 11:8), as Jesus did (cf. Mk 3:5), as God does in the face of injustice (cf. Am 2:4–8; 5:7–12; Ps 106:40). It is not good for us to become inured to evil; it is not good when our

social consciousness is dulled before "an exploitation that is leaving destruction and even death throughout our region ... jeopardizing the lives of millions of people and especially the habitat of peasants and indigenous peoples."[11] The incidents of injustice and cruelty that took place in the Amazon region even in the last century ought to provoke profound abhorrence, but they should also make us more sensitive to the need to acknowledge current forms of human exploitation, abuse, and killing. With regard to the shameful past, let us listen, for example, to an account of the sufferings of the indigenous people during the "rubber age" in the Venezuelan Amazon region: "They gave no money to the indigenous people, but only merchandise, for which they charged dearly and the people never finished paying for it. ... They would pay for it but they were told, 'You are racking up a debt,' and the indigenous person would have to go back to work. ... More than twenty ye'kuana towns were entirely razed to the ground. The ye'kuana women were raped and their breasts amputated, pregnant women had their children torn from the womb, men had their fingers or hands cut off so they could not sail ... along with other scenes of the most absurd sadism."[12]

16. Such a history of suffering and contempt does not heal easily. Nor has colonization ended; in many places, it has been changed, disguised, and concealed,[13] while losing none of its contempt for the life of the poor and the fragility of the environment. As the bishops of the Brazilian Amazon have noted, "the history of the Amazon region shows that it was always a minority that profited from the poverty of the majority and from the

unscrupulous plundering of the region's natural riches, God's gift to the peoples who have lived there for millennia and to the immigrants who arrived in centuries past."[14]

17. Yet even as we feel this healthy sense of indignation, we are reminded that it is possible to overcome the various colonizing mentalities and to build networks of solidarity and development. "The challenge, in short, is to ensure a globalization in solidarity, a globalization without marginalization."[15] Alternatives can be sought for sustainable herding and agriculture, sources of energy that do not pollute, dignified means of employment that do not entail the destruction of the natural environment and of cultures. At the same time, the indigenous peoples and the poor need to be given an education suited to developing their abilities and empowering them. These are the goals to which the genuine talent and shrewdness of political leaders should be directed. Not as a way of restoring to the dead the life taken from them, or even of compensating the survivors of that carnage, but at least today to be authentically human.

18. It is encouraging to remember that amid the grave excesses of the colonization of the Amazon region, so full of "contradictions and suffering,"[16] many missionaries came to bring the Gospel, leaving their homes and leading an austere and demanding life alongside those who were most defenseless. We know that not all of them were exemplary, yet the work of those who remained faithful to the Gospel also inspired "a legislation like the Laws of the Indies, which defended the dignity of

the indigenous peoples from violence against their peoples and territories."[17] Since it was often the priests who protected the indigenous peoples from their plunderers and abusers, the missionaries recounted that "they begged insistently that we not abandon them and they extorted from us the promise that we would return."[18]

19. Today the Church can be no less committed. She is called to hear the plea of the Amazonian peoples and "to exercise with transparency her prophetic mission."[19] At the same time, since we cannot deny that the wheat was mixed with the tares, and that the missionaries did not always take the side of the oppressed, I express my shame and once more "I humbly ask forgiveness, not only for the offenses of the Church herself, but for the crimes committed against the native peoples during the so-called conquest of America"[20] as well as for the terrible crimes that followed throughout the history of the Amazon region. I thank the members of the original peoples and I repeat: "Your lives cry out. ... You are living memory of the mission that God has entrusted to us all: the protection of our common home."[21]

A sense of community

20. Efforts to build a just society require a capacity for fraternity, a spirit of human fellowship. Hence, without diminishing the importance of personal freedom, it is clear that the original peoples of the Amazon region have a strong sense of community. It permeates "their work, their rest, their relationships, their rites and celebrations. Everything is shared; private areas — typical of modernity — are minimal. Life is a communal jour-

ney where tasks and responsibilities are apportioned and shared on the basis of the common good. There is no room for the notion of an individual detached from the community or from the land."[22] Their relationships are steeped in the surrounding nature, which they feel and think of as a reality that integrates society and culture, and a prolongation of their bodies, personal, familial, and communal:

> "The morning star draws near,
> the wings of the hummingbirds flutter;
> my heart pounds louder than the cascade:
> with your lips I will water the land
> as the breeze softly blows among us."[23]

21. All this makes even more unsettling the sense of bewilderment and uprootedness felt by those indigenous people who feel forced to migrate to the cities, as they attempt to preserve their dignity amid more individualistic urban habitats and a hostile environment. How do we heal all these hurts, how do we bring serenity and meaning to these uprooted lives? Given situations like these we ought to appreciate and accompany the efforts made by many of those groups to preserve their values and way of life, and to integrate in new situations without losing them, but instead offering them as their own contribution to the common good.

22. Christ redeemed the whole person, and he wishes to restore in each of us the capacity to enter into relationship with others. The Gospel proposes the divine charity welling up in the heart of Christ and generating a pur-

suit of justice that is at once a hymn of fraternity and of solidarity, an impetus to the culture of encounter. The wisdom of the way of life of the original peoples — for all its limitations — encourages us to deepen this desire. In view of this, the bishops of Ecuador have appealed for "a new social and cultural system which privileges fraternal relations within a framework of acknowledgment and esteem for the different cultures and ecosystems, one capable of opposing every form of discrimination and oppression between human beings."[24]

Broken institutions

23. In the encyclical *Laudato Si'*, I noted that "if everything is related, then the health of the society's institutions has consequences for the environment and the quality of human life. ... Within each social stratum, and between them, institutions develop to regulate human relationships. Anything which weakens those institutions has negative consequences, such as injustice, violence, and loss of freedom. A number of countries have a relatively low level of institutional effectiveness, which results in greater problems for their people."[25]

24. Where do the institutions of civil society in the Amazon region stand? The synod's *Instrumentum Laboris*, which synthesizes contributions made by numerous individuals and groups from the Amazon region, speaks of "a culture that poisons the state and its institutions, permeating all social strata, including the indigenous communities. We are talking about a true moral scourge; as a result, there is a loss of confidence in institutions and their representatives, which totally discredits politics

and social organizations. The Amazonian peoples are not immune to corruption, and they end up being its principal victims."[26]

25. Nor can we exclude the possibility that members of the Church have been part of networks of corruption, at times to the point of agreeing to keep silent in exchange for economic assistance for ecclesial works. Precisely for this reason, proposals were made at the synod to insist that "special attention be paid to the provenance of donations or other kinds of benefits, as well as to investments made by ecclesiastical institutions or individual Christians."[27]

Social dialogue

26. The Amazon region ought to be a place of social dialogue, especially between the various original peoples, for the sake of developing forms of fellowship and joint struggle. The rest of us are called to participate as "guests" and to seek out with great respect paths of encounter that can enrich the Amazon region. If we wish to dialogue, we should do this in the first place with the poor. They are not just another party to be won over, or merely another individual seated at a table of equals. They are our principal dialogue partners, those from whom we have the most to learn, to whom we need to listen out of a duty of justice, and from whom we must ask permission before presenting our proposals. Their words, their hopes, and their fears should be the most authoritative voice at any table of dialogue on the Amazon region. And the great question is: "What is their idea of 'good living' for themselves and for those who will come after them?"

27. Dialogue must not only favor the preferential option on behalf of the poor, the marginalized and the excluded, but also respect them as having a leading role to play. Others must be acknowledged and esteemed precisely *as others*, each with his or her own feelings, choices, and ways of living and working. Otherwise, the result would be, once again, "a plan drawn up by the few for the few,"[28] if not "a consensus on paper or a transient peace for a contented minority."[29] Should this be the case, "a prophetic voice must be raised,"[30] and we as Christians are called to make it heard.

This gives rise to the following dream.

CHAPTER TWO

...

A CULTURAL DREAM

28. The important thing is to promote the Amazon region, but this does not imply colonizing it culturally, but instead helping it to bring out the best of itself. That is in fact what education is meant to do: to cultivate without uprooting, to foster growth without weakening identity, to be supportive without being invasive. Just as there are potentialities in nature that could be lost forever, something similar could happen with cultures that have a message yet to be heard but are now more than ever under threat.

The Amazonian polyhedron

29. The Amazon region is host to many peoples and nationalities, and over 110 indigenous peoples in voluntary isolation (IPVI).[31] Their situation is very tenuous and many feel that they are the last bearers of a treasure doomed to disappear, allowed to survive only if they make no trouble, while the postmodern colonization advances. They should not be viewed as "uncivilized" savages. They are simply heirs to different cultures and other forms of civilization that in earlier times were quite developed.[32]

30. Prior to the colonial period, the population was concentrated on the shores of the rivers and lakes, but the advance of colonization drove the older inhabitants into the interior of the forest. Today, growing desertification once more drives many of them into the outskirts and sidewalks of the cities, at times in dire poverty but also in an inner fragmentation due to the loss of the values that had previously sustained them. There they usually lack the points of reference and the cultural roots that provided them with an identity and a sense of dignity, and they swell the ranks of the outcast. This disrupts the cultural transmission of a wisdom that had been passed down for centuries from generation to generation. Cities, which should be places of encounter, of mutual enrichment and of exchange between different cultures, become a tragic scenario of discarded lives.

31. Each of the peoples that has survived in the Amazon region possesses its own cultural identity and unique richness in our multicultural universe, thanks to the close relationship established by the inhabitants with their surroundings in a non-deterministic symbiosis which is hard to conceive using mental categories imported from without:

> "Once there was a countryside, with its river,
> its animals, its clouds and its trees.
> But sometimes, when the countryside, with its
>   river and trees,
> was nowhere to be seen,
> those things had to spring up in the mind of a
>   child."[33]

"Make the river your blood ...
Then plant yourself,
blossom and grow:
let your roots sink into the ground
forever and ever,
and then at last
become a canoe,
a skiff, a raft,
soil, a jug,
a farmhouse, and a man."[34]

32. Human groupings, their lifestyles, and their world-views, are as varied as the land itself, since they have had to adapt themselves to geography and its possibilities. Fishers are not the same as hunters, and the gatherers of the interior are not the same as those who cultivate the flood lands. Even now, we see in the Amazon region thousands of indigenous communities, people of African descent, river people and city dwellers, who differ from one another and embrace a great human diversity. In each land and its features, God manifests himself and reflects something of his inexhaustible beauty. Each distinct group, then, in a vital synthesis with its surroundings, develops its own form of wisdom. Those of us who observe this from without should avoid unfair generalizations, simplistic arguments, and conclusions drawn only on the basis of our own mindsets and experiences.

Caring for roots
33. Here I would like to point out that "a consumerist vision of human beings, encouraged by the mechanisms

of today's globalized economy, has a leveling effect on cultures, diminishing the immense variety which is the heritage of all humanity."[35] This especially affects young people, for it has a tendency to "blur what is distinctive about their origins and backgrounds, and turn them into a new line of malleable goods."[36] In order to prevent this process of human impoverishment, there is a need to care lovingly for our roots, since they are "a fixed point from which we can grow and meet new challenges."[37] I urge the young people of the Amazon region, especially the indigenous peoples, to "take charge of your roots, because from the roots comes the strength that will make you grow, flourish, and bear fruit."[38] For those of them who are baptized, these roots include the history of the people of Israel and the Church up to our own day. Knowledge of them can bring joy and, above all, a hope capable of inspiring noble and courageous actions.

34. For centuries, the Amazonian peoples passed down their cultural wisdom orally, with myths, legends, and tales, as in the case of "those primitive storytellers who traversed the forests bringing stories from town to town, keeping alive a community which, without the umbilical cord of those stories, distance and lack of communication would have fragmented and dissolved."[39] That is why it is important "to let older people tell their long stories"[40] and for young people to take the time to drink deeply from that source.

35. Although there is a growing risk that this cultural richness will be lost; thanks be to God, in recent years

some peoples have taken to writing down their stories and describing the meaning of their customs. In this way, they themselves can explicitly acknowledge that they possess something more than an ethnic identity and that they are bearers of precious personal, family, and collective memories. I am pleased to see that people who have lost contact with their roots are trying to recover their damaged memory. Then too, the professional sectors have seen a growing sense of Amazonian identity; even for people who are the descendants of immigrants, the Amazon region has become a source of artistic, literary, musical, and cultural inspiration. The various arts, and poetry in particular, have found inspiration in its water, its forests, its seething life, as well as its cultural diversity and its ecological and social challenges.

Intercultural encounter

36. Like all cultural realities, the cultures of the interior Amazon region have their limits. Western urban cultures have them as well. Factors like consumerism, individualism, discrimination, inequality, and any number of others represent the weaker side of supposedly more developed cultures. The ethnic groups that, in interaction with nature, developed a cultural treasure marked by a strong sense of community, readily notice our darker aspects, which we do not recognize in the midst of our alleged progress. Consequently, it will prove beneficial to listen to their experience of life.

37. Starting from our roots, let us sit around the common table, a place of conversation and of shared hopes. In this

way our differences, which could seem like a banner or a wall, can become a bridge. Identity and dialogue are not enemies. Our own cultural identity is strengthened and enriched as a result of dialogue with those unlike ourselves. Nor is our authentic identity preserved by an impoverished isolation. Far be it from me to propose a completely enclosed, historical, static "indigenism" that would reject any kind of blending (*mestizaje*). A culture can grow barren when it "becomes inward-looking, and tries to perpetuate obsolete ways of living by rejecting any exchange or debate with regard to the truth about man."[41] That would be unrealistic, since it is not easy to protect oneself from cultural invasion. For this reason, interest and concern for the cultural values of the indigenous groups should be shared by everyone, for their richness is also our own. If we ourselves do not increase our sense of co-responsibility for the diversity that embellishes our humanity, we can hardly demand that the groups from the interior forest be uncritically open to "civilization."

38. In the Amazon region, even between the different original peoples, it is possible to develop "intercultural relations where diversity does not mean threat, and does not justify hierarchies of power of some over others, but dialogue between different cultural visions, of celebration, of interrelationship, and of revival of hope."[42]

Endangered cultures, peoples at risk
39. The globalized economy shamelessly damages human, social, and cultural richness. The disintegration of families that comes about as a result of forced migra-

tions affects the transmission of values, for "the family is and has always been the social institution that has most contributed to keeping our cultures alive."[43] Furthermore, "faced with a colonizing invasion of means of mass communication," there is a need to promote for the original peoples "alternative forms of communication based on their own languages and cultures" and for "the indigenous subjects themselves [to] become present in already existing means of communication."[44]

40. In any project for the Amazon region, "there is a need to respect the rights of peoples and cultures and to appreciate that the development of a social group presupposes a historical process which takes place within a cultural context and demands the constant and active involvement of local people from within their own culture. Nor can the notion of the quality of life be imposed from without, for quality of life must be understood within the world of symbols and customs proper to each human group."[45] If the ancestral cultures of the original peoples arose and developed in intimate contact with the natural environment, then it will be hard for them to remain unaffected once that environment is damaged.

This leads us to the next dream.

CHAPTER THREE

...

AN ECOLOGICAL DREAM

41. In a cultural reality like the Amazon region, where there is such a close relationship between human beings and nature, daily existence is always cosmic. Setting others free from their forms of bondage surely involves caring for the environment and defending it,[46] but, even more, helping the human heart to be open with trust to the God who not only has created all that exists but has also given us himself in Jesus Christ. The Lord, who is the first to care for us, teaches us to care for our brothers and sisters and the environment which he daily gives us. This is the first ecology that we need.

In the Amazon region, one better understands the words of Benedict XVI when he said that "alongside the ecology of nature, there exists what can be called a 'human' ecology which in turn demands a 'social' ecology. All this means that humanity ... must be increasingly conscious of the links between natural ecology, or respect for nature, and human ecology."[47] This insistence that "everything is connected"[48] is particularly true of a territory like the Amazon region.

42. If the care of people and the care of ecosystems are inseparable, this becomes especially important in places where "the forest is not a resource to be exploited; it is a being, or various beings, with which we have to relate."[49] The wisdom of the original peoples of the Amazon region "inspires care and respect for creation, with a clear consciousness of its limits, and prohibits its abuse. To abuse nature is to abuse our ancestors, our brothers and sisters, creation and the Creator, and to mortgage the future."[50] When the indigenous peoples "remain on their land, they themselves care for it best,"[51] provided that they do not let themselves be taken in by the siren songs and the self-serving proposals of power groups. The harm done to nature affects those peoples in a very direct and verifiable way, since, in their words, "we are water, air, earth and life of the environment created by God. For this reason, we demand an end to the mistreatment and destruction of mother Earth. The land has blood, and it is bleeding; the multinationals have cut the veins of our mother Earth."[52]

This dream made of water

43. In the Amazon region, water is queen; the rivers and streams are like veins, and water determines every form of life:

"There, in the dead of summer, when the last gusts from the East subside in the still air, the hydrometer takes the place of the thermometer in determining the weather. Lives depend on a painful alternation of falls and rises in the level of the great rivers. These always swell in an impressive manner. The Amazonas overflows its bed and in just a few days raises the level of its waters. ... The flooding puts a stop to everything. Caught in the dense foliage of the *igarapies*, man awaits with rare stoicism the inexorable end of that paradoxical winter of elevated temperatures. The receding of the waters is summer. It is the resurrection of the primitive activity of those who carry on with the only form of life compatible with the unequal extremes of nature that make the continuation of any effort impossible."[53]

44. The shimmering water of the great Amazon River collects and enlivens all its surroundings:

> "Amazonas,
> capital of the syllables of water,
> father and patriarch, you are
> the hidden eternity
> of the processes of fertilization;
> streams alight upon you like birds."[54]

45. The Amazon is also the spinal column that creates harmony and unity: "the river does not divide us. It unites us and helps us live together amid different cultures and languages."[55] While it is true that in these lands there are many "Amazon regions," the principal axis is the great river, the offspring of many rivers:

"From the high mountain range where the snows are eternal, the water descends and traces a shimmering line along the ancient skin of the rock: the Amazon is born. It is born every second. It descends slowly, a sinuous ray of light, and then swells in the lowland. Rushing upon green spaces, it invents its own path and expands. Underground waters well up to embrace the water that falls from the Andes. From the belly of the pure white clouds, swept by the wind, water falls from heaven. It collects and advances, multiplied in infinite pathways, bathing the immense plain. ... This is the Great Amazonia, covering the humid tropic with its astonishingly thick forest, vast reaches untouched by man, pulsing with life threading through its deep waters. ... From the time that men have lived there, there has arisen from the depths of its waters, and running through the heart of its forest, a terrible fear: that its life is slowly but surely coming to an end."[56]

46. Popular poets, enamored of its immense beauty, have tried to express the feelings this river evokes and the life that it bestows as it passes amid a dance of dolphins, anacondas, trees, and canoes. Yet they also lament the dangers that menace it. Those poets, contemplatives and prophets, help free us from the technocratic and consumerist paradigm that destroys nature and robs us of a truly dignified existence:

"The world is suffering from its feet being turned into rubber, its legs into leather, its body into cloth and its head into steel. ... The world is suffering from its trees being turned into rifles, its ploughshares into tanks, as the image of the sower scattering seed yields to the tank with its flamethrower, which sows only deserts. Only poetry, with its humble voice, will be able to save this world."[57]

The cry of the Amazon region

47. Poetry helps give voice to a painful sensation shared by many of us today. The inescapable truth is that, as things stand, this way of treating the Amazon territory spells the end for so much life, for so much beauty, even though people would like to keep thinking that nothing is happening:

> "Those who thought that the river was only a
>   piece of rope,
> a plaything, were mistaken.
> The river is a thin vein on the face of the earth ...
> The river is a cord enclosing animals and trees.
> If pulled too tight, the river could burst.
> It could burst and spatter our faces with water
>   and blood."[58]

48. The equilibrium of our planet also depends on the health of the Amazon region. Together with the biome of the Congo and Borneo, it contains a dazzling diversity of woodlands on which rain cycles, climate balance, and a great variety of living beings also depend. It serves as a great filter of carbon dioxide, which helps avoid the warming of the earth. For the most part, its surface is poor in topsoil, with the result that the forest "really grows on the soil and not from the soil."[59] When the forest is eliminated, it is not replaced, because all that is left is a terrain with few nutrients that then turns into a dry land or one poor in vegetation. This is quite serious, since the interior of the Amazonian forest contains countless resources that could prove essential for curing diseases. Its fish, fruit, and other abundant gifts

35

provide rich nutrition for humanity. Furthermore, in an ecosystem like that of the Amazon region, each part is essential for the preservation of the whole. The lowlands and marine vegetation also need to be fertilized by the alluvium of the Amazon. The cry of the Amazon region reaches everyone because "the conquest and exploitation of resources ... has today reached the point of threatening the environment's hospitable aspect: the environment as 'resource' risks threatening the environment as 'home.'"[60] The interest of a few powerful industries should not be considered more important than the good of the Amazon region and of humanity as a whole.

49. It is not enough to be concerned about preserving the most visible species in danger of extinction. There is a crucial need to realize that "the good functioning of ecosystems also requires fungi, algae, worms, insects, reptiles, and an innumerable variety of microorganisms. Some less numerous species, although generally unseen, nonetheless play a critical role in maintaining the equilibrium of a particular place."[61] This is easily overlooked when evaluating the environmental impact of economic projects of extraction, energy, timber, and other industries that destroy and pollute. So too, the water that abounds in the Amazon region is an essential good for human survival, yet the sources of pollution are increasing.[62]

50. Indeed, in addition to the economic interests of local businesspersons and politicians, there also exist "huge global economic interests."[63] The answer is not

to be found, then, in "internationalizing" the Amazon region,[64] but rather in a greater sense of responsibility on the part of national governments. In this regard, "we cannot fail to praise the commitment of international agencies and civil society organizations which draw public attention to these issues and offer critical co-operation, employing legitimate means of pressure, to ensure that each government carries out its proper and inalienable responsibility to preserve its country's environment and natural resources, without capitulating to spurious local or international interests."[65]

51. To protect the Amazon region, it is good to combine ancestral wisdom with contemporary technical knowledge, always working for a sustainable management of the land while also preserving the lifestyle and value systems of those who live there.[66] They, particularly the original peoples, have a right to receive — in addition to basic education — thorough and straightforward information about projects, their extent and their consequences and risks, in order to be able to relate that information to their own interests and their own knowledge of the place, and thus to give or withhold their consent, or to propose alternatives.[67]

52. The powerful are never satisfied with the profits they make, and the resources of economic power greatly increase as a result of scientific and technological advances. For this reason, all of us should insist on the urgent need to establish "a legal framework which can set clear boundaries and ensure the protection of ecosystems ... otherwise, the new power structures based

on the techno-economic paradigm may overwhelm not only our politics, but also freedom and justice."[68] If God calls us to listen both to the cry of the poor and that of the earth,[69] then for us, "the cry of the Amazon region to the Creator is similar to the cry of God's people in Egypt (cf. Ex 3:7). It is a cry of slavery and abandonment pleading for freedom."[70]

The prophecy of contemplation

53. Frequently we let our consciences be deadened, since "distractions constantly dull our realization of just how limited and finite our world really is."[71] From a superficial standpoint, we might well think that "things do not look that serious, and the planet could continue as it is for some time. Such evasiveness serves as a license to carrying on with our present lifestyles and models of production and consumption. This is the way human beings contrive to feed their self-destructive vices: trying not to see them, trying not to acknowledge them, delaying the important decisions and pretending that nothing will happen."[72]

54. In addition, I would also observe that each distinct species has a value in itself, yet "each year sees the disappearance of thousands of plant and animal species which we will never know, which our children will never see, because they have been lost forever. The great majority become extinct for reasons related to human activity. Because of us, thousands of species will no longer give glory to God by their very existence, nor convey their message to us. We have no such right."[73]

55. From the original peoples, we can learn to *contemplate* the Amazon region and not simply analyze it, and thus appreciate this precious mystery that transcends us. We can *love* it, not simply use it, with the result that love can awaken a deep and sincere interest. Even more, we can *feel intimately a part of it* and not only defend it; then the Amazon region will once more become like a mother to us. For "we do not look at the world from without but from within, conscious of the bonds with which the Father has linked us to all beings."[74]

56. Let us awaken our God-given aesthetic and contemplative sense that so often we let languish. Let us remember that "if someone has not learned to stop and admire something beautiful, we should not be surprised if he or she treats everything as an object to be used and abused without scruple."[75] On the other hand, if we enter into communion with the forest, our voices will easily blend with its own and become a prayer: "as we rest in the shade of an ancient eucalyptus, our prayer for light joins in the song of the eternal foliage."[76] This interior conversion will enable us to weep for the Amazon region and to join in its cry to the Lord.

57. Jesus said: "Are not five sparrows sold for two pennies? Yet not one of them is forgotten in God's sight" (Lk 12:6). God our Father, who created each being in the universe with infinite love, calls us to be his means for hearing the cry of the Amazon region. If we respond to this heart-rending plea, it will become clear that the creatures of the Amazon region are not forgotten by our heavenly Father. For Christians, Jesus himself cries out

to us from their midst, "because the risen One is mysteriously holding them to himself and directing them towards fullness as their end. The very flowers of the field and the birds which his human eyes contemplated and admired are now imbued with his radiant presence."[77] For all these reasons, we believers encounter in the Amazon region a theological locus, a space where God himself reveals himself and summons his sons and daughters.

Ecological education and habits

58. In this regard, we can take one step further and note that an integral ecology cannot be content simply with fine-tuning technical questions or political, juridical, and social decisions. The best ecology always has an educational dimension that can encourage the development of new habits in individuals and groups. Sadly, many of those living in the Amazon region have acquired habits typical of the larger cities, where consumerism and the culture of waste are already deeply rooted. A sound and sustainable ecology, one capable of bringing about change, will not develop unless people are changed, unless they are encouraged to opt for another style of life, one less greedy and more serene, more respectful and less anxious, more fraternal.

59. Indeed, "the emptier a person's heart is, the more he or she needs things to buy, own, and consume. It becomes almost impossible to accept the limits imposed by reality. ... Our concern cannot be limited merely to the threat of extreme weather events, but must also extend to the catastrophic consequences of social unrest.

Obsession with a consumerist lifestyle, above all when few people are capable of maintaining it, can only lead to violence and mutual destruction."[78]

60. The Church, with her broad spiritual experience, her renewed appreciation of the value of creation, her concern for justice, her option for the poor, her educational tradition, and her history of becoming incarnate in so many different cultures throughout the world, also desires to contribute to the protection and growth of the Amazon region.

This leads to the next dream, which I would like to share more directly with the Catholic pastors and faithful.

CHAPTER FOUR

•••

AN ECCLESIAL DREAM

61. The Church is called to journey alongside the people of the Amazon region. In Latin America, this journey found privileged expression at the Bishops' Conference in Medellin (1968) and its application to the Amazon region at Santarem (1972),[79] followed by Puebla (1979), Santo Domingo (1992), and Aparecida (2007). The journey continues, and missionary efforts, if they are to develop a Church with an Amazonian face, need to grow in a culture of encounter towards "a multifaceted harmony."[80] But for this incarnation of the Church and the Gospel to be possible, the great missionary proclamation must continue to resound.

The message that needs to be heard in the Amazon region

62. Recognizing the many problems and needs that cry out from the heart of the Amazon region, we can respond beginning with organizations, technical resources, opportunities for discussion and political programs: All these can be part of the solution. Yet as Christians, we cannot set aside the call to faith that we have received from the Gospel. In our desire to struggle side by

side with everyone, we are not ashamed of Jesus Christ. Those who have encountered him, those who live as his friends and identify with his message, must inevitably speak of him and bring to others his offer of new life: "Woe to me if I do not preach the Gospel!" (1 Cor 9:16).

63. An authentic option for the poor and the abandoned, while motivating us to liberate them from material poverty and to defend their rights, also involves inviting them to a friendship with the Lord that can elevate and dignify them. How sad it would be if they were to receive from us a body of teachings or a moral code, but not the great message of salvation, the missionary appeal that speaks to the heart and gives meaning to everything else in life. Nor can we be content with a social message. If we devote our lives to their service, to working for the justice and dignity that they deserve, we cannot conceal the fact that we do so because we see Christ in them and because we acknowledge the immense dignity that they have received from God, the Father who loves them with boundless love.

64. They have a right to hear the Gospel, and above all that first proclamation, the *kerygma*, which is "the principal proclamation, the one which we must hear again and again in different ways, the one which we must announce one way or another."[81] It proclaims a God who infinitely loves every man and woman and has revealed this love fully in Jesus Christ, crucified for us and risen in our lives. I would ask that you re-read the brief summary of this "great message" found in chapter four of the exhortation *Christus Vivit*. That message, expressed in a

variety of ways, must constantly resound in the Amazon region. Without that impassioned proclamation, every ecclesial structure would become just another NGO and we would not follow the command given us by Christ: "Go into all the world and preach the Gospel to the whole creation" (Mk 16:15).

65. Any project for growth in the Christian life needs to be centered continually on this message, for "all Christian formation consists of entering more deeply into the kerygma."[82] The fundamental response to this message, when it leads to a personal encounter with the Lord, is fraternal charity, "the new commandment, the first and the greatest of the commandments, and the one that best identifies us as Christ's disciples."[83] Indeed, the kerygma and fraternal charity constitute the great synthesis of the whole content of the Gospel, to be proclaimed unceasingly in the Amazon region. That is what shaped the lives of the great evangelizers of Latin America, like Saint Turibius of Mogrovejo or Saint Joseph of Anchieta.

Inculturation

66. As she perseveres in the preaching of the kerygma, the Church also needs to grow in the Amazon region. In doing so, she constantly reshapes her identity through listening and dialogue with the people, the realities, and the history of the lands in which she finds herself. In this way, she is able to engage increasingly in a necessary process of inculturation that rejects nothing of the goodness that already exists in Amazonian cultures, but brings it to fulfilment in the light of the Gospel.[84] Nor does she scorn the richness of Christian wisdom hand-

ed down through the centuries, presuming to ignore the history in which God has worked in many ways. For the Church has a varied face, "not only in terms of space ... but also of time."[85] Here we see the authentic Tradition of the Church, which is not a static deposit or a museum piece, but the root of a constantly growing tree.[86] This millennial Tradition bears witness to God's work in the midst of his people and "is called to keep the flame alive rather than to guard its ashes."[87]

67. Saint John Paul II taught that in proposing the Gospel message, "the Church does not intend to deny the autonomy of culture. On the contrary, she has the greatest respect for it," since culture "is not only an object of redemption and elevation but can also play a role of mediation and cooperation."[88] Addressing indigenous peoples of America, he reminded them that "a faith that does not become culture is a faith not fully accepted, not fully reflected upon, not faithfully lived."[89] Cultural challenges invite the Church to maintain "a watchful and critical attitude," while at the same time showing "confident attention."[90]

68. Here I would reiterate what I stated about inculturation in the apostolic exhortation *Evangelii Gaudium*, based on the conviction that "grace supposes culture, and God's gift becomes flesh in the culture of those who receive it."[91] We can see that it involves a double movement. On the one hand, a fruitful process takes place when the Gospel takes root in a given place, for "whenever a community receives the message of salvation, the Holy Spirit enriches its culture with the transforming power of the

Gospel."[92] On the other hand, the Church herself undergoes a process of reception that enriches her with the fruits of what the Spirit has already mysteriously sown in that culture. In this way, "the Holy Spirit adorns the Church, showing her new aspects of revelation and giving her a new face."[93] In the end, this means allowing and encouraging the inexhaustible riches of the Gospel to be preached "in categories proper to each culture, creating a new synthesis with that particular culture."[94]

69. "The history of the Church shows that Christianity does not have simply one cultural expression,"[95] and "we would not do justice to the logic of the incarnation if we thought of Christianity as monocultural and monotonous."[96] There is a risk that evangelizers who come to a particular area may think that they must not only communicate the Gospel but also the culture in which they grew up, failing to realize that it is not essential "to impose a specific cultural form, no matter how beautiful or ancient it may be."[97] What is needed is courageous openness to the novelty of the Spirit, who is always able to create something new with the inexhaustible riches of Jesus Christ. Indeed, "inculturation commits the Church to a difficult but necessary journey."[98] True, "this is always a slow process and that we can be overly fearful," ending up as "mere onlookers as the Church gradually stagnates."[99] But let us be fearless; let us not clip the wings of the Holy Spirit.

Paths of inculturation in the Amazon region
70. For the Church to achieve a renewed inculturation of the Gospel in the Amazon region, she needs to listen

to its ancestral wisdom, listen once more to the voice of its elders, recognize the values present in the way of life of the original communities, and recover the rich stories of its peoples. In the Amazon region, we have inherited great riches from the pre-Columbian cultures. These include "openness to the action of God, a sense of gratitude for the fruits of the earth, the sacred character of human life and esteem for the family, a sense of solidarity and shared responsibility in common work, the importance of worship, belief in a life beyond this earth, and many other values."[100]

71. In this regard, the indigenous peoples of the Amazon region express the authentic quality of life as "good living." This involves personal, familial, communal, and cosmic harmony and finds expression in a communitarian approach to existence, the ability to find joy and fulfillment in an austere and simple life, and a responsible care of nature that preserves resources for future generations. The aboriginal peoples give us the example of a joyful sobriety and in this sense, "they have much to teach us."[101] They know how to be content with little; they enjoy God's little gifts without accumulating great possessions; they do not destroy things needlessly; they care for ecosystems and they recognize that the earth, while serving as a generous source of support for their life, also has a maternal dimension that evokes respect and tender love. All these things should be valued and taken up in the process of evangelization.[102]

72. While working for them and with them, we are called "to be their friends, to listen to them, to speak for them

and to embrace the mysterious wisdom which God wishes to share with us through them."[103] Those who live in cities need to appreciate this wisdom and to allow themselves to be "re-educated" in the face of frenzied consumerism and urban isolation. The Church herself can be a means of assisting this cultural retrieval through a precious synthesis with the preaching of the Gospel. She can also become a sign and means of charity, inasmuch as urban communities must be missionary not only to those in their midst but also to the poor who, driven by dire need, arrive from the interior and are welcomed. In the same way, these communities can stay close to young migrants and help them integrate into the city without falling prey to its networks of depravity. All these forms of ecclesial outreach, born of love, are valuable contributions to a process of inculturation.

73. Inculturation elevates and fulfills. Certainly, we should esteem the indigenous mysticism that sees the interconnection and interdependence of the whole of creation, the mysticism of gratuitousness that loves life as a gift, the mysticism of a sacred wonder before nature, and all its forms of life.

At the same time, though, we are called to turn this relationship with God present in the cosmos into an increasingly personal relationship with a "Thou" who sustains our lives and wants to give them a meaning, a "Thou" who knows us and loves us:

"Shadows float from me, dead wood.
But the star is born without reproach

over the expert hands of this child,
that conquer the waters and the night.
It has to be enough for me to know
that you know me
completely, from before my days."[104]

74. Similarly, a relationship with Jesus Christ, true God and true man, liberator, and redeemer, is not inimical to the markedly cosmic worldview that characterizes the indigenous peoples, since he is also the Risen Lord who permeates all things.[105] In Christian experience, "all the creatures of the material universe find their true meaning in the incarnate Word, for the Son of God has incorporated in his person part of the material world, planting in it a seed of definitive transformation."[106] He is present in a glorious and mysterious way in the river, the trees, the fish, and the wind, as the Lord who reigns in creation without ever losing his transfigured wounds, while in the Eucharist he takes up the elements of this world and confers on all things the meaning of the paschal gift.

Social and spiritual inculturation
75. Given the situation of poverty and neglect experienced by so many inhabitants of the Amazon region, inculturation will necessarily have a markedly social cast, accompanied by a resolute defense of human rights; in this way it will reveal the face of Christ, who "wished with special tenderness to be identified with the weak and the poor."[107] Indeed, "from the heart of the Gospel we see the profound connection between evangelization and human advancement."[108] For Christian com-

munities, this entails a clear commitment to the justice of God's kingdom through work for the advancement of those who have been "discarded." It follows that a suitable training of pastoral workers in the Church's social doctrine is most important.

76. At the same time, the inculturation of the Gospel in the Amazon region must better integrate the social and the spiritual, so that the poor do not have to look outside the Church for a spirituality that responds to their deepest yearnings. This does not mean an alienating and individualistic religiosity that would silence social demands for a more dignified life, but neither does it mean ignoring the transcendent and spiritual dimension, as if material development alone were sufficient for human beings. We are thus called not merely to join those two things, but to connect them at a deeper level. In this way, we will reveal the true beauty of the Gospel, which fully humanizes, integrally dignifies persons and peoples, and brings fulfilment to every heart and the whole of life.

Starting points for an Amazonian holiness
77. This will give rise to witnesses of holiness with an Amazonian face, not imitations of models imported from other places. A holiness born of encounter and engagement, contemplation and service, receptive solitude and life in community, cheerful sobriety and the struggle for justice. A holiness attained by "each individual in his or her own way,"[109] but also by peoples, where grace becomes incarnate and shines forth with distinctive features. Let us imagine a holiness with Amazonian

features, called to challenge the universal Church.

78. A process of inculturation involving not only individuals but also peoples demands a respectful and understanding love for those peoples. This process has already begun in much of the Amazon region. More than forty years ago, the bishops of the Peruvian Amazon pointed out that in many of the groups present in that region, those to be evangelized, shaped by a varied and changing culture, have been "initially evangelized." As a result, they possess "certain features of popular Catholicism that, perhaps originally introduced by pastoral workers, are now something that the people have made their own, even changing their meaning and handing them down from generation to generation."[110] Let us not be quick to describe as superstition or paganism certain religious practices that arise spontaneously from the life of peoples. Rather, we ought to know how to distinguish the wheat growing alongside the tares, for "popular piety can enable us to see how the faith, once received, becomes embodied in a culture and is constantly passed on."[111]

79. It is possible to take up an indigenous symbol in some way, without necessarily considering it as idolatry. A myth charged with spiritual meaning can be used to advantage and not always considered a pagan error. Some religious festivals have a sacred meaning and are occasions for gathering and fraternity, albeit in need of a gradual process of purification or maturation. A missionary of souls will try to discover the legitimate needs and concerns that seek an outlet in at times imperfect,

partial, or mistaken religious expressions, and will attempt to respond to them with an inculturated spirituality.

80. Such a spirituality will certainly be centered on the one God and Lord, while at the same time in contact with the daily needs of people who strive for a dignified life, who want to enjoy life's blessings, to find peace and harmony, to resolve family problems, to care for their illnesses, and to see their children grow up happy. The greatest danger would be to prevent them from encountering Christ by presenting him as an enemy of joy or as someone indifferent to human questions and difficulties.[112] Nowadays, it is essential to show that holiness takes nothing away from our "energy, vitality, or joy."[113]

The inculturation of the liturgy

81. The inculturation of Christian spirituality in the cultures of the original peoples can benefit in a particular way from the sacraments, since they unite the divine and the cosmic, grace and creation. In the Amazon region, the sacraments should not be viewed in discontinuity with creation. They "are a privileged way in which nature is taken up by God to become a means of mediating supernatural life."[114] They are the fulfillment of creation, in which nature is elevated to become a locus and instrument of grace, enabling us "to embrace the world on a different plane."[115]

82. In the Eucharist, God, "in the culmination of the mystery of the Incarnation, chose to reach our intimate depths through a fragment of matter." The Eucharist

"joins heaven and earth; it embraces and penetrates all creation."[116] For this reason, it can be a "motivation for our concerns for the environment, directing us to be stewards of all creation."[117] In this sense, "encountering God does not mean fleeing from this world or turning our back on nature."[118] It means that we can take up into the liturgy many elements proper to the experience of indigenous peoples in their contact with nature, and respect native forms of expression in song, dance, rituals, gestures, and symbols. The Second Vatican Council called for this effort to inculturate the liturgy among indigenous peoples;[119] over fifty years have passed and we still have far to go along these lines.[120]

83. On Sunday, "Christian spirituality incorporates the value of relaxation and festivity. [Nowadays] we tend to demean contemplative rest as something unproductive and unnecessary, but this is to do away with the very thing which is most important about work: its meaning. We are called to include in our work a dimension of receptivity and gratuity."[121] Aboriginal peoples are familiar with this gratuity and this healthy contemplative leisure. Our celebrations should help them experience this in the Sunday liturgy and encounter the light of God's word and the Eucharist, which illumines our daily existence.

84. The sacraments reveal and communicate the God who is close and who comes with mercy to heal and strengthen his children. Consequently, they should be accessible, especially for the poor, and must never be refused for financial reasons. Nor is there room, in

the presence of the poor and forgotten of the Amazon region, for a discipline that excludes and turns people away, for in that way they end up being discarded by a Church that has become a toll-house. Rather, "in such difficult situations of need, the Church must be particularly concerned to offer understanding, comfort and acceptance, rather than imposing straightaway a set of rules that only lead people to feel judged and abandoned by the very Mother called to show them God's mercy."[122] For the Church, mercy can become a mere sentimental catchword unless it finds concrete expression in her pastoral outreach.[123]

Inculturation of forms of ministry

85. Inculturation should also be increasingly reflected in an incarnate form of ecclesial organization and ministry. If we are to inculturate spirituality, holiness, and the Gospel itself, how can we not consider an inculturation of the ways we structure and carry out ecclesial ministries? The pastoral presence of the Church in the Amazon region is uneven, due in part to the vast expanse of the territory, its many remote places, its broad cultural diversity, its grave social problems, and the preference of some peoples to live in isolation. We cannot remain unconcerned; a specific and courageous response is required of the Church.

86. Efforts need to be made to configure ministry in such a way that it is at the service of a more frequent celebration of the Eucharist, even in the remotest and most isolated communities. At Aparecida, all were asked to heed the lament of the many Amazonian communi-

ties "deprived of the Sunday Eucharist for long periods of time."[124] There is also a need for ministers who can understand Amazonian sensibilities and cultures from within.

87. The way of shaping priestly life and ministry is not monolithic; it develops distinctive traits in different parts of the world. This is why it is important to determine what is most specific to a priest, what cannot be delegated. The answer lies in the Sacrament of Holy Orders, which configures him to Christ the priest. The first conclusion, then, is that the exclusive character received in holy orders qualifies the priest alone to preside at the Eucharist.[125] That is his particular, principal, and non-delegable function. There are those who think that what distinguishes the priest is power, the fact that he is the highest authority in the community. Yet Saint John Paul II explained that, although the priesthood is considered "hierarchical," this function is not meant to be superior to the others, but rather is "totally ordered to the holiness of Christ's members."[126] When the priest is said to be a sign of "Christ the head," this refers principally to the fact that Christ is the source of all grace: He is the head of the Church because "he has the power of pouring out grace upon all the members of the Church."[127]

88. The priest is a sign of that head and wellspring of grace above all when he celebrates the Eucharist, the source and summit of the entire Christian life.[128] That is his great power, a power that can only be received in the Sacrament of Holy Orders. For this reason, only the priest can say: "This is *my* body." There are other words

too, that he alone can speak: "I absolve you from your sins." Because sacramental forgiveness is at the service of a worthy celebration of the Eucharist. These two sacraments lie at the heart of the priest's exclusive identity.[129]

89. In the specific circumstances of the Amazon region, particularly in its forests and more remote places, a way must be found to ensure this priestly ministry. The laity can proclaim God's word, teach, organize communities, celebrate certain sacraments, seek different ways to express popular devotion, and develop the multitude of gifts that the Spirit pours out in their midst. But they need the celebration of the Eucharist because it "makes the Church."[130] We can even say that "no Christian community is built up which does not grow from and hinge on the celebration of the most holy Eucharist."[131] If we are truly convinced that this is the case, then every effort should be made to ensure that the Amazonian peoples do not lack this food of new life and the sacrament of forgiveness.

90. This urgent need leads me to urge all bishops, especially those in Latin America, not only to promote prayer for priestly vocations, but also to be more generous in encouraging those who display a missionary vocation to opt for the Amazon region.[132] At the same time, it is appropriate that the structure and content of both initial and ongoing priestly formation be thoroughly revised, so that priests can acquire the attitudes and abilities demanded by dialogue with Amazonian cultures. This formation must be preeminently pastoral and favor

the development of priestly mercy.[133]

Communities filled with life

91. The Eucharist is also the great sacrament that signifies and realizes the Church's *unity*.[134] It is celebrated "so that from being strangers, dispersed and indifferent to ... another, we may become united, equals and friends."[135] The one who presides at the Eucharist must foster communion, which is not just any unity, but one that welcomes the abundant variety of gifts and charisms that the Spirit pours out upon the community.

92. The Eucharist, then, as source and summit, requires the development of that rich variety. Priests are necessary, but this does not mean that permanent deacons (of whom there should be many more in the Amazon region), religious women and lay persons cannot regularly assume important responsibilities for the growth of communities, and perform those functions ever more effectively with the aid of a suitable accompaniment.

93. Consequently, it is not simply a question of facilitating a greater presence of ordained ministers who can celebrate the Eucharist. That would be a very narrow aim, were we not also to strive to awaken new life in communities. We need to promote an encounter with God's word and growth in holiness through various kinds of lay service that call for a process of education — biblical, doctrinal, spiritual, and practical — and a variety of programs of ongoing formation.

94. A Church of Amazonian features requires the stable

presence of mature and lay leaders endowed with authority[136] and familiar with the languages, cultures, spiritual experience, and communal way of life in the different places, but also open to the multiplicity of gifts that the Holy Spirit bestows on everyone. For wherever there is a particular need, he has already poured out the charisms that can meet it. This requires the Church to be open to the Spirit's boldness, to trust in, and concretely to permit, the growth of a specific ecclesial culture that is *distinctively lay*. The challenges in the Amazon region demand of the Church a special effort to be present at every level, and this can only be possible through the vigorous, broad, and active involvement of the laity.

95. Many consecrated persons have devoted their energies and a good part of their lives in service to the kingdom of God in Amazonia. The consecrated life, as capable of dialogue, synthesis, incarnation, and prophecy, has a special place in this diverse and harmonious configuration of the Church in the Amazon region. But it needs a new impetus to inculturation, one that would combine creativity, missionary boldness, sensitivity, and the strength typical of community life.

96. Base communities, when able to combine the defense of social rights with missionary proclamation and spirituality, have been authentic experiences of synodality in the Church's journey of evangelization in the Amazon region. In many cases they "have helped form Christians committed to their faith, disciples and missionaries of the Lord, as is attested by the generous commitment of so many of their members, even to the point

of shedding their blood."[137]

97. I encourage the growth of the collaborative efforts being made through the Pan Amazonian Ecclesial Network and other associations to implement the proposal of Aparecida to "establish a collaborative ministry among the local churches of the various South American countries in the Amazon basin, with differentiated priorities."[138] This applies particularly to relations between Churches located on the borders between nations.

98. Finally, I would note that we cannot always plan projects with stable communities in mind, because the Amazonian region sees a great deal of internal mobility, constant and frequently pendular migration; "the region has effectively become a migration corridor."[139] "Transhumance in the Amazon has not been well understood or sufficiently examined from the pastoral standpoint."[140] Consequently, thought should be given to itinerant missionary teams and "support provided for the presence and mobility of consecrated men and women closest to those who are most impoverished and excluded."[141] This is also a challenge for our urban communities, which ought to come up with creative and generous ways, especially on the outskirts, to be close and welcoming to families and young people who arrive from the interior.

The strength and gift of women
99. In the Amazon region, there are communities that have long preserved and handed on the Faith even though no priest has come their way, even for decades.

This could happen because of the presence of strong and generous women who, undoubtedly called and prompted by the Holy Spirit, baptized, catechized, prayed, and acted as missionaries. For centuries, women have kept the Church alive in those places through their remarkable devotion and deep faith. Some of them, speaking at the synod, moved us profoundly by their testimony.

100. This summons us to broaden our vision, lest we restrict our understanding of the Church to her functional structures. Such a reductionism would lead us to believe that women would be granted a greater status and participation in the Church only if they were admitted to holy orders. But that approach would in fact narrow our vision; it would lead us to clericalize women, diminish the great value of what they have already accomplished, and subtly make their indispensable contribution less effective.

101. Jesus Christ appears as the spouse of the community that celebrates the Eucharist through the figure of a man who presides as a sign of the one priest. This dialogue between the spouse and his bride, which arises in adoration and sanctifies the community, should not trap us in partial conceptions of power in the Church. The Lord chose to reveal his power and his love through two human faces: the face of his divine Son made man and the face of a creature, a woman, Mary. Women make their contribution to the Church in a way that is properly theirs, by making present the tender strength of Mary, the Mother. As a result, we do not limit ourselves to a functional approach, but enter instead into

the inmost structure of the Church. In this way, we will fundamentally realize why without women the Church breaks down, and how many communities in the Amazon would have collapsed, had women not been there to sustain them, keep them together, and care for them. This shows the kind of power that is typically theirs.

102. We must keep encouraging those simple and straightforward gifts that enabled women in the Amazon region to play so active a role in society, even though communities now face many new and unprecedented threats. The present situation requires us to encourage the emergence of other forms of service and charisms that are proper to women and responsive to the specific needs of the peoples of the Amazon region at this moment in history.

103. In a synodal Church, those women who in fact have a central part to play in Amazonian communities should have access to positions, including ecclesial services, that do not entail holy orders and that can better signify the role that is theirs. Here it should be noted that these services entail stability, public recognition, and a commission from the bishop. This would also allow women to have a real and effective impact on the organization, the most important decisions and the direction of communities, while continuing to do so in a way that reflects their womanhood.

Expanding horizons beyond conflicts
104. It often happens that in particular places pastoral workers envisage very different solutions to the problems they face, and consequently propose apparently

opposed forms of ecclesial organization. When this occurs, it is probable that the real response to the challenges of evangelization lies in transcending the two approaches and finding other, better ways, perhaps not yet even imagined. Conflict is overcome at a higher level, where each group can join the other in a new reality, while remaining faithful to itself. Everything is resolved "on a higher plane and preserves what is valid and useful on both sides."[142] Otherwise, conflict traps us; "we lose our perspective, our horizons shrink and reality itself begins to fall apart."[143]

105. In no way does this mean relativizing problems, fleeing from them, or letting things stay as they are. Authentic solutions are never found by dampening boldness, shirking concrete demands, or assigning blame to others. On the contrary, solutions are found by "overflow," that is, by transcending the contraposition that limits our vision and recognizing a greater gift that God is offering. From that new gift, accepted with boldness and generosity, from that unexpected gift which awakens a new and greater creativity, there will pour forth as from an overflowing fountain the answers that contraposition did not allow us to see. In its earliest days, the Christian Faith spread remarkably in accordance with this way of thinking, which enabled it, from its Jewish roots, to take shape in the Greco-Roman cultures, and in time to acquire distinctive forms. Similarly, in this historical moment, the Amazon region challenges us to transcend limited perspectives and "pragmatic" solutions mired in partial approaches, in order to seek paths of inculturation that are broader and bolder.

Ecumenical and interreligious coexistence

106. In an Amazonian region characterized by many religions, we believers need to find occasions to speak to one another and to act together for the common good and the promotion of the poor. This has nothing to do with watering down or concealing our deepest convictions when we encounter others who think differently than ourselves. If we believe that the Holy Spirit can work amid differences, then we will try to let ourselves be enriched by that insight, while embracing it from the core of our own convictions and our own identity. For the deeper, stronger, and richer that identity is, the more we will be capable of enriching others with our own proper contribution.

107. We Catholics possess in sacred Scripture a treasure that other religions do not accept, even though at times they may read it with interest and even esteem some of its teachings. We attempt to do something similar with the sacred texts of other religions and religious communities, which contain "precepts and doctrines that ... often reflect a ray of that truth which enlightens all men and women."[144] We also possess a great treasure in the seven sacraments, which some Christian communities do not accept in their totality or in the same sense. At the same time that we believe firmly in Jesus as the sole Redeemer of the world, we cultivate a deep devotion to his Mother. Even though we know that this is not the case with all Christian confessions, we feel it [is] our duty to share with the Amazon region the treasure of that warm, maternal love which we ourselves have received. In fact, I will conclude this exhortation with a

few words addressed to Mary.

108. None of this needs to create enmity between us. In a true spirit of dialogue, we grow in our ability to grasp the significance of what others say and do, even if we cannot accept it as our own conviction. In this way, it becomes possible to be frank and open about our beliefs, while continuing to discuss, to seek points of contact, and above all, to work and struggle together for the good of the Amazon region. The strength of what unites all of us as Christians is supremely important. We can be so attentive to what divides us that at times we no longer appreciate or value what unites us. And what unites us is what lets us remain in this world without being swallowed up by its immanence, its spiritual emptiness, its complacent selfishness, its consumerist and self-destructive individualism.

109. All of us, as Christians, are united by faith in God, the Father who gives us life and loves us so greatly. We are united by faith in Jesus Christ, the one Savior, who set us free by his precious blood and his glorious resurrection. We are united by our desire for his word that guides our steps. We are united by the fire of the Spirit, who sends us forth on mission. We are united by the new commandment that Jesus left us, by the pursuit of the civilization of love and by passion for the kingdom that the Lord calls us to build with him. We are united by the struggle for peace and justice. We are united by the conviction that not everything ends with this life, but that we are called to the heavenly banquet, where God will wipe away every tear and take up all that we

did for those who suffer.

110. All this unites us. How can we not struggle togeth-er? How can we not pray and work together, side by side, to defend the poor of the Amazon region, to show the sacred countenance of the Lord, and to care for his work of creation?

CONCLUSION

•••

MOTHER OF THE AMAZON REGION

111. After sharing a few of my dreams, I encourage everyone to advance along concrete paths that can allow the reality of the Amazon region to be transformed and set free from the evils that beset it. Let us now lift our gaze to Mary. The Mother whom Christ gave us is also the one Mother of all, who reveals herself in the Amazon region in distinct ways. We know that "the indigenous peoples have a vital encounter with Jesus Christ in many ways; but the path of Mary has contributed greatly to this encounter."[145] Faced with the marvel of the Amazon region, which we discovered ever more fully during the preparation and celebration of the synod, I consider it best to conclude this exhortation by turning to her:

Mother of life,
in your maternal womb Jesus took flesh,
the Lord of all that exists.
Risen, he transfigured you by his light
and made you the Queen of all creation.
For that reason, we ask you, Mary, to reign
in the beating heart of Amazonia.

CONCLUSION

Show yourself the Mother of all creatures,
in the beauty of the flowers, the rivers,
the great river that courses through it,
and all the life pulsing in its forests.
Tenderly care for this explosion of beauty.

Ask Jesus to pour out all his love
on the men and women who dwell there,
that they may know how to appreciate
     and care for it.

Bring your Son to birth in their hearts,
so that he can shine forth in the Amazon region,
in its peoples and in its cultures,
by the light of his word,
by his consoling love,
by his message of fraternity and justice.

And at every Eucharist,
may all this awe and wonder be lifted up
to the glory of the Father.

Mother, look upon the poor of the Amazon
     region,
for their home is being destroyed by petty
     interests.
How much pain and misery,
how much neglect and abuse there is
in this blessed land
overflowing with life!

Touch the hearts of the powerful,

for, even though we sense that the hour is late,
you call us to save
what is still alive.

Mother whose heart is pierced,
who yourself suffer in your mistreated sons and
daughters,
and in the wounds inflicted on nature,
reign in the Amazon,
together with your Son.
Reign so that no one else can claim lordship
over the handiwork of God.

We trust in you, Mother of life.
Do not abandon us
in this dark hour.

Amen.

Given in Rome, at the Cathedral of Saint John Lateran, on February 2, the Feast of the Presentation of the Lord, in the year 2020, the seventh of my Pontificate.

FRANCISCUS

NOTES

1 Encyclical Letter *Laudato Si'* (24 May 2015), 49: AAS 107 (2015), 866.

2 *Instrumentum Laboris*, 45.

3 Ana Varela Tafur, "Timareo," in *Lo que no veo en visiones*, Lima, 1992.

4 Jorge Vega Márquez, "Amazonia solitária," in *Poesía obrera*, Cobija-Pando-Bolivia, 2009, 39.

5 Red Eclesial Panamazónica (REPAM), Brazil, *Síntesis del aporte al Sínodo*, 120; cf. *Instrumentum Laboris*, 45.

6 *Address to Young People*, São Paulo, Brazil (10 May 2007), 2.

7 Cf. Alberto C. Araújo, "Imaginario amazónico," in *Amazonia real: amazoniareal.com.br* (29 January 2014).

8 Saint Paul VI, Encyclical Letter *Populorum Progressio* (26 March 1967), 57: AAS 59 (1967), 285.

9 Saint John Paul II, *Address to the Pontifical Academy of Social Sciences* (27 April 2001), 4: AAS 93 (2001), 600.

10 Cf. *Instrumentum Laboris*, 41.

11 Fifth General Conference of the Latin American and Caribbean Bishops, *Aparecida Document* (29 June 2007), 473.

12 Ramón Iribertegui, *Amazonas: El hombre y el caucho*, ed. Vicariato Apostólico de Puerto Ayacucho-Venezuela, Monografía n. 4, Caracas, 1987, 307ff.

13 Cf. Amarílis Tupiassú, "Amazônia, das travessias lusitanas à literatura de até agora," in *Estudos Avançados* vol. 19, n. 53, São Paulo (Jan./Apr. 2005): "In effect, after the end of the first colonization, the Amazon region continued to be an area subject to age-old greed, now under new rhetorical guises ... on the part of "civilizing" agents who did not even need to be personified in order to generate and multiply the new faces of the old decimation, now through a slow death."

NOTES

14 Bishops of the Brazilian Amazon Region, *Carta al Pueblo de Dios*, Santarem-Brazil (6 July 2012).

15 Saint John Paul II, *Message for the 1998 World Day of Peace*, 3: AAS 90 (1998), 150.

16 Third General Conference of the Latin American and Caribbean Bishops, *Puebla Document* (23 March 1979), 6.

17 *Instrumentum Laboris*, 6. Pope Paul III, in his the Brief *Veritas Ipsa* (2 June 1537), condemned racist theses and recognized that the native peoples, whether Christian or not, possess the dignity of the human person, enjoy the right to their possessions and may not be reduced to slavery. The Pope declared: "as truly men ... are by no means to be deprived of their liberty or the possession of their property, even though they be outside the faith of Jesus Christ." This magisterial teaching was reaffirmed by Popes Gregory XIV, Bull *Cum Sicuti* (28 April 1591); Urban VIII, Bull *Commissum Nobis* (22 April 1639); Benedict XIV Bull *Immensa Pastorum Principis* to the Bishops of Brazil (20 December 1741); Gregory XVI, Brief *In Supremo* (3 December 1839); Leo XIII, *Epistle to the Bishops of Brazil on Slavery* (15 May 1888); and Saint John Paul II, *Message to the Indigenous People of America*, Santo Domingo (12 October 1992), 2: *Insegnamenti* 15/2 (1982), 346.

18 Frederico Benício de Sousa Costa, *Pastoral Letter (1909)*. Ed. Imprenta del gobierno del estado de Amazonas, Manaus, 1994, 83.

19 *Instrumentum Laboris*, 7.

20 *Address at the Second World Meeting of Popular Movements*, Santa Cruz de la Sierra-Bolivia (9 July 2015).

21 *Address at the Meeting with Indigenous People of Amazonia*, Puerto Maldonado-Peru (19 January 2018): AAS 110 (2018), 300.

22 *Instrumentum Laboris*, 24.

23 Yana Lucila Lema, *Tamyahuan Shamakupani (Con la lluvia estoy viviendo)*, 1, at http://siwarmayu.com/es/yana-lucila-lema-6-poemas-de-tamyawan-shamukupani-con-la-lluvia-estoy-viviendo.

24 Bishops' Conference of Ecuador, *Cuidemos nuestro planeta* (20 April 2012), 3.

72

25 No. 142: AAS 107 (2015), 904-905.

26 No. 82.

27 Ibid., 83.

28 Apostolic Exhortation *Evangelii Gaudium* (24 November 2013), 239: AAS 105 (2013), 1116.

29 Ibid., 218: AAS 105 (2013), 1110.

30 Ibid.

31 Cf. *Instrumentum Laboris*, 57.

32 Cf. Evaristo Eduardo de Miranda, *Quando o Amazonas corria para o Pacifico*, Petrópolis, 2007, 83-93.

33 Juan Carlos Galeano, "Paisajes," in *Amazonia y otros poemas*, ed. Universidad Externado de Colombia, Bogotá, 2011, 31.

34 Javier Yglesias, "Llamado," in *Revista peruana de literatura*, n. 6 (June 2007), 31.

35 Encyclical Letter *Laudato Si'* (24 May 2015), 144: AAS 107 (2015) 905.

36 Post-Synodal Apostolic Exhortation *Christus Vivit* (25 March 2019), 186.

37 Ibid., 200.

38 *Videomessage for the World Indigenous Youth Gathering*, Soloy-Panama (18 January 2019).

39 Mario Vargas Llosa, Prologue to *El Hablador*, Madrid (8 October 2007).

40 Post-Synodal Apostolic Exhortation *Christus Vivit* (25 March 2019), 195.

41 Saint John Paul II, Encyclical Letter *Centesimus Annus* (1 May 1991), 50: AAS 83 (1991), 856.

42 Fifth General Conference of the Latin American and Caribbean Bishops, *Aparecida Document* (29 June 2007), 97.

43 *Address at the Meeting with Indigenous People of Amazonia*, Puerto Maldonado-Peru (19 January 2018): AAS 110 (2018), 301.

NOTES

44 *Instrumentum Laboris*, 123, e.

45 Encyclical Letter *Laudato Si'* (24 May 2015), 144: AAS 107 (2015), 906.

46 Cf. Benedict XVI, Encyclical Letter *Caritas in veritate* (29 June 2009), 51: AAS 101 (2009), 687: "Nature, especially in our time, is so integrated into the dynamics of society and culture that by now it hardly constitutes an independent variable. Desertification and the decline in productivity in some agricultural areas are also the result of impoverishment and underdevelopment among their inhabitants."

47 *Message for the 2007 World Day of Peace*, 8: *Insegnamenti*, II/2 (2006), 776.

48 Encyclical Letter *Laudato Si'* (24 May 2015), 16, 91, 117, 138, 240: AAS 107 (2015), 854, 884, 894, 903, 941.

49 Document *Bolivia: informe país. Consulta pre sinodal*, 2019, p. 36; cf. *Instrumentum Laboris*, 23.

50 *Instrumentum Laboris*, 26.

51 Encyclical Letter *Laudato Si'* (24 May 2015), 146: AAS 107 (2015), 906.

52 *Documento con aportes al Sínodo de la Diócesis de San José del Guaviare y de la Arquidiócesis de Villavicencio y Granada* (Colombia); cf. *Instrumentum Laboris*, 17.

53 Euclides da Cunhae, *Los Sertones (Os Sertões)*, Buenos Aires (1946), 65-66.

54 Pablo Neruda, "Amazonas" in *Canto General* (1938), I, IV.

55 REPAM, Document *Eje de Fronteras*. Preparación para el Sínodo de la Amazonia, Tabatinga-Brasil (3 February 2019), p. 3; cf. *Instrumentum Laboris*, 8.

56 Amadeu Thiago de Lello, *Amazonas, patria da agua*. Spanish translation by Jorge Timossi, in http://letras-uruguay .espaciolatino.com/aaa/mello_thiago/amazonas_patria_da _agua.htm.

57 Vinicius de Moraes, *Para vivir un gran amor*, Buenos Aires,

NOTES

2013, 166.

58 Juan Carlos Galeano, "Los que creyeron," in *Amazonia y otros poemas*, ed. Universidad externado de Colombia, Bogotá, 2011, 44.

59 Harald Sioli, *A Amazônia*, Petropolis (1985), 60.

60 Saint John Paul II, *Address to an International Convention on "The Environment and Health"* (24 March 1997), 2.

61 Encyclical Letter *Laudato Si'* (24 May 2015), 34: AAS 107 (2015), 860.

62 Cf. ibid., 28-31: AAS 107 (2015), 858-859.

63 Ibid., 38: AAS 107 (2015), 862.

64 Cf. Fifth General Conference of the Latin American and Caribbean Bishops, *Aparecida Document* (29 June 2007), 86.

65 Encyclical Letter *Laudato Si'* (24 May 2015), 38: AAS 107 (2015), 862.

66 Cf. ibid, 144, 187: AAS 107 (2015), 905-906, 921.

67 Cf. ibid., 183: AAS 107 (2015), 920.

68 Ibid., 53: AAS 107 (2015), 868.

69 Cf. ibid., 49: AAS 107 (2015), 866.

70 *Preparatory Document for the Synod on the Pan Amazon Region*, 8.

71 Encyclical Letter *Laudato Si'* (24 May 2015), 56: AAS 107 (2015), 869.

72 Ibid., 59: AAS 107 (2015), 870.

73 Ibid., 33: AAS 107 (2015), 860.

74 Ibid, 220: AAS 107 (2015), 934.

75 Ibid., 215: AAS 107 (2015), 932.

76 Sui Yun, *Cantos para el mendigo y el rey*, Wiesbaden, 2000.

77 Encyclical Letter *Laudato Si'* (24 May 2015), 100: AAS 107 (2015), 887.

78 Ibid., 204: AAS 107 (2015), 928.

79 Cf. Documents of Santarem (1972) and Manaos (1997) in National Conference of the Bishops of Brazil, *Desafío missionário. Documentos da Igreja na Amazônia*, Brasilia, 2014, pp. 9-28 and 67-84.

80 Cf. Apostolic Exhortation *Evangelii Gaudium* (24 November 2013), 220: AAS 105 (2013), 1110.

81 Ibid., 164: AAS 105 (2013), 1088-1089.

82 Ibid., 165: AAS 105 (2013), 1089.

83 Ibid., 161: AAS 105 (2013), 1087.

84 As the Second Vatican Council states in No. 44 of the Constitution *Gaudium et Spes*: "The Church learned early in her history to express the Christian message in the concepts and languages of different peoples and tried to clarify it in the light of the wisdom of their philosophers: it was an attempt to adapt the Gospel to the understanding of all and the requirements of the learned, insofar as this could be done. Indeed, this kind of adaptation and preaching of the revealed word must ever be the law of all evangelization. In this way it is possible to create in every country the possibility of expressing the message of Christ in suitable terms and to foster vital contact and exchange between the Church and different cultures."

85 *Letter to the Pilgrim People of God in Germany*, 29 June 2019, 9: *L'Osservatore Romano*, 1-2 July 2019, p. 9.

86 Cf. Saint Vincent of Lerins, *Commonitorium primum*, cap. 23: PL 50, 668: "Ut annis scilicet consolidetur, dilatetur tempore, sublimetur aetate."

87 *Letter to the Pilgrim People of God in Germany*, 29 June 2019, 9. Cf. the words attributed to Gustav Mahler: "Tradition ist nicht die Anbetung der Asche, sondern die Weitergabe des Feuers": "Tradition is not the worship of ashes but the passing on of the flame."

88 *Address to University Professors and Cultural Leaders*, Coimbra (15 May 1982): *Insegnamenti* 5/2 (1982), 1702-1703.

89 *Message to the Indigenous Peoples of the American Continent*, Santo Domingo (12 October 1992), 6: *Insegnamenti* 15/2 (1992),

346; cf. *Address to Participants in the National Congress of the Ecclesial Movement of Cultural Commitment* (16 January 1982), 2: *Insegnamenti* 5/1 (1982), 131.

90 Saint John Paul II, Post-Synodal Apostolic Exhortation *Vita Consecrata* (15 March 1996), 98: AAS 88 (1996), 474-475.

91 No. 115: AAS 105 (2013),1068.

92 Ibid., 116: AAS 105 (2013),1068.

93 Ibid.

94 Ibid., 129: AAS 105 (2013), 1074.

95 Ibid., 116: AAS 105 (2013), 1068.

96 Ibid., 117: AAS 105 (2013), 1069.

97 Ibid.

98 Saint John Paul II, *Address to the Plenary Assembly of the Pontifical Council for Culture* (17 January 1987): *Insegnamenti* 10/1 (1987), 125.

99 Apostolic Exhortation *Evangelii Gaudium* (24 November 2013), 129: AAS 105 (2013), 1074.

100 Fourth General Meeting of the Latin American and Caribbean Episcopate, *Santo Domingo Document* (12-28 October 1992), 17.

101 Apostolic Exhortation *Evangelii Gaudium* (24 November 2013), 198: AAS 105 (2013), 1103.

102 Cf. Vittorio Messori-Joseph Ratzinger, *Rapporto sulla fede*, Cinisello Balsamo, 1985, 211-212.

103 Apostolic Exhortation *Evangelii Gaudium* (24 November 2013), 198: AAS 105 (2013), 1103.

104 Pedro Casaldáliga, "Carta de navegar (*Por el Tocantins amazónico*)" in *El tiempo y la espera*, Santander, 1986.

105 Saint Thomas Aquinas explains it in this way: "The threefold way that God is in things: one is common, by essence, presence and power; another by grace in his saints; a third in Christ, by union" (*Ad Colossenses*, II, 2).

106 Encyclical Letter *Laudato Si'* (24 May 2015), 235: AAS 107

(2015), 939.

107 Third General Meeting of the Latin American and Caribbean Episcopate, *Puebla Document* (23 March 1979), 196.

108 Apostolic Exhortation *Evangelii Gaudium* (24 November 2013), 178: AAS 105 (2013), 1094.

109 Second Vatican Ecumenical Council, Dogmatic Constitution on the Church *Lumen Gentium*, 11; cf. Apostolic Exhortation *Gaudete et Exsultate* (19 March 2018), 10-11.

110 Apostolic Vicariates of the Peruvian Amazon, "Segunda asamblea episcopal regional de la selva," San Ramón-Perú (5 October 1973), in *Éxodo de la Iglesia en la Amazonia. Documentos pastorales de la Iglesia en la Amazonia peruana*, Iquitos, 1976, 121.

111 Apostolic Exhortation *Evangelii Gaudium* (24 November 2013), 123: AAS 105 (2013), 1071.

112 Cf. Apostolic Exhortation *Gaudete et Exsultate* (19 March 2018), 126-127.

113 Ibid., 32.

114 Encyclical Letter *Laudato Si'* (24 May 2015), 235: AAS 107 (2015), 939.

115 Ibid.

116 Ibid., 236: AAS 107 (2015), 940.

117 Ibid.

118 Ibid., 235: AAS 107 (2015), 939.

119 Cf. Constitution on the Sacred Liturgy *Sacrosanctum Concilium*, 37-40, 65, 77, 81.

120 During the Synod, there was a proposal to develop an "Amazonian rite."

121 Encyclical Letter *Laudato Si'* (24 May 2015), 237: AAS 107 (2015), 940.

122 Apostolic Exhortation *Amoris Laetitia* (19 March 2016), 49: AAS 108 (2016), 331; cf. ibid. 305: AAS 108 (2016), 436-437.

123 Cf. ibid., 296, 308: AAS 108 (2016), 430-431, 438.

NOTES

124 Fifth General Conference of the Latin American and Caribbean Bishops, *Aparecida Document*, 29 June 2007, 100 e.

125 Cf. Congregation for the Doctrine of the Faith, Letter *Sacerdotium Ministeriale* to Bishops of the Catholic Church on certain questions concerning the minister of the Eucharist (6 August 1983): AAS 75 (1983), 1001-1009.

126 Apostolic Letter *Mulieris Dignitatem* (15 August 1988), 27: AAS 80 (1988), 1718.

127 Saint Thomas Aquinas, *Summa Theologiae* III, q. 8, a.1, resp.

128 Cf. Second Vatican Ecumenical Council, Decree on the Ministry and Life of Priests *Presbyterorum Ordinis*, 5; Saint John Paul II, Encyclical Letter *Ecclesia de Eucharistia* (17 April 2003), 26: AAS 95 (2003), 448.

129 It is also proper to the priest to administer the Anointing of the Sick, because it is intimately linked to the forgiveness of sins: "And if he has committed sins, he will be forgiven" (*Jas* 5:15).

130 *Catechism of the Catholic Church*, 1396; SAINT JOHN PAUL II, Encyclical Letter *Ecclesia de Eucharistia* (17 April 2003), 26: AAS 95 (2003), 451; cf. HENRI DE LUBAC, *Meditation sur l'Église*, Paris (1968), 101.

131 Second Vatican Ecumenical Council, Decree on the Ministry and Life of Priests *Presbyterorum Ordinis*, 6.

132 It is noteworthy that, in some countries of the Amazon Basin, more missionaries go to Europe or the United States than remain to assist their own Vicariates in the Amazon region.

133 At the Synod, mention was also made of the lack of seminaries for the priestly formation of indigenous people.

134 Cf. Second Vatican Ecumenical Council, Dogmatic Constitution on the Church *Lumen Gentium*, 3.

135 Saint Paul VI, *Homily on the Solemnity of Corpus Christi*, 17 June 1965: *Insegnamenti* 3 (1965), 358.

136 It is possible that, due to a lack of priests, a bishop can entrust "participation in the exercise of the pastoral care of a parish ... to a deacon, to another person who is not a priest, or to a community of

persons" (*Code of Canon Law*, 517 §2).

137 Fifth General Conference of the Latin American and Caribbean Bishops, *Aparecida Document*, 29 June 2007, 178.

138 Ibid., 475.

139 *Instrumentum Laboris*, 65.

140 Ibid., 63.

141 Ibid., 129, d, 2.

142 Apostolic Exhortation *Evangelii Gaudium* (24 November 2013), 228: AAS 105 (2013), 1113.

143 Ibid., 226: AAS 105 (2013), 1112.

144 Second Vatican Ecumenical Council, Declaration on the Relation of the Church to Non-Christian Religions *Nostra Aetate*, 2.

145 CELAM, *III Simposio latinoamericano sobre Teología India*, Ciudad de Guatemala (23-27 October 2006).